There Is No Sound In My Scream

Drugs, Truth, and Faith

Kimberly E. Mallory

To my son, Bernard Mallory, who is my heart beat.
To my sister, Deborah Mallory, who is my lifeline and has been by my side through my entire journey.
To my Mentor and Spiritual Counselor, Dr. Sylathia Hollie.
To my Coach and Publisher, Reverend Rita M. Henderson, CEO of Five Fold Publishing LLC.

To everyone that believed in me.

Contents

Introduction..1

Trusting and Believing 1

Chapter 1 3

In the Beginning 3

Chapter 2 13

There's No Place like Home 13

Chapter 3 17

Best Friends for Life...17

Chapter 4 23

Drugs Got the Best of Me 23

Chapter 5 47

Learning How to Live Again 47

Chapter 6 54

Life without Drugs 54

Chapter 7 62

Trust the Process...62

About the Author 67

Introduction

Trusting and Believing

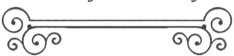

I was awakened early one morning, and I kept hearing God telling me to write this book, but I just turned over and went back to sleep. Only to continue to keep getting awakened around that same time every morning. There was so much doubt and fear, and I found myself asking God, why should someone like me write a book? Where do I even start? God said from the beginning. All while ignoring the answers God gave me to my questions, I just couldn't seem to wrap my mind around writing a book until one morning while lying in bed, God spoke to me and said, "Write this book because I told you to!" God told me that, "Not only will you help others with your story; writing this book will allow you to finally heal what you've been suppressing for many years."I began having this sense of peace about writing my book and said to God, "God I'm ready."

God had instructed me to have a pen and notebook on my nightstand. A week or so went by, and I told God I was ready, but I hadn't heard Him speak back to me. I could just imagine the look on God's face telling Him I'm ready as if He was supposed to jump and say okay. But while I was in that waiting period, that sense of ambivalence set in. I remember just looking up and saying, "God, I trust you even though I hadn't heard from you in weeks."I asked Him to forgive me for not being obedient when He first told me to write this book. I cried out to Him, asking not to forget me. When I woke up one morning to get ready for work, God spoke to me and said the name of my book would be **"There Is No Sound In My Scream."** I hurriedly wrote down the title just as He told me. He continued to speak to me, and eventually gave me the titles of seven chapters.

This book was birthed in prayers for you, dear reader. As you read this book, may God help you to understand that your past does not determine what God has intended you to be. You do not have to stay in a life of abuse and drugs. May God heal and deliver those who are currently going through or have experienced the guilt and shame that comes with this. I also pray that this book comes to you in all truth and honesty. Amen.

Chapter 1

In the Beginning

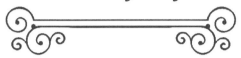

Somebody help me!!! My life is spiraling out of control. Can anybody hear me? There's a voice telling me that no one can help me. Where is everybody? Why isn't anyone helping me? How can anybody hear me if no one is listening?

I was two years old when the doctors told my mother she only had 6 months to live. However, because of my mother's determination to live, she lived 9 years later. But unfortunately, the cancer came back and began to spread throughout her body. She lost her battle with cancer, and she passed away. I felt so alone after her death. I remember grabbing my father's razor and running to the basement sitting on the floor as I cut both of my wrists. Blood was everywhere, and all I could remember was lying in a hospital talking to a Psychiatrist. They didn't keep me for long. I was later diagnosed as being depressed because of my mom's death.

Shortly after

"Daddy, why are you packing me and my sister Debbie's clothes? Where are we going? I don't understand what is happening right now." At that moment, it seemed like my whole life was turning upside down. Next thing I knew, I was getting off of a plane in Florida with a woman, a man, and some kids who we were told were relatives, meeting me and my sister at the airport gate. I walked outside, and all I could see was beautiful palm trees. I was full of smiles thinking to myself, "Wow! This is not so bad." And the weather, coming from Michigan, was better than I could ever imagine.

My sister and I had moved into a house where there were already 9 other children, not to mention two adults, which made 13 people in one house. But I have to admit, I couldn't stop smiling, seeing so many kids in one house. Thinking to myself, this is going to be a lot of fun living here, and just maybe it may help me forget that I no longer have my mother. I quickly learned that you could not judge a book by its cover because, in a blink of an eye, my life turned into a nightmare. My smile became a frown, and my joy became constant tears.

My relative didn't like me much, and she made it clear to me from the time I walked in the door. Why does she hate me so much? What did I ever do to her? She told me that I reminded her of my mother and that she hates me, so if I reminded her of my mother, was she saying that she hates my mother as well? It was beyond me why my mother said on her death bed that she wants our relative to take care of my sister and me.

I could not understand what kind of person tells an 11-year-old child that they hate them and that they will never amount to anything in life? This became something that she told me regularly to the point where I began to believe what she said. Although I began missing my friends back home, I knew I had no choice but to make the best of a bad situation. But wait, what really is the best since I've been here in Florida, I don't know what best is. All I can remember is the slightest things I would do; I would get in trouble and be punished. I was put in a dark closet, and that was after I was beaten, which was my punishment.

Every day became a day just to survive the thoughts of suicide. Days became weeks, weeks became months and months became years, and I came to the realization that it was normal to feel suicidal, it was normal for me to feel worthless. It became apparent to me that I was only living here to take up space, as I was reminded that as well. I had nothing else to compare my life to other than pain, tears, and a heavy heart full of sadness.

I didn't know much about God, but for some reason, I found myself asking Him "why God?", "God, why did my mother die?" "God, why is this happening to me?" "God, do you hate me too?" I never got any answers back from God, maybe I did, maybe I didn't and if God was actually real, how could He allow me to go through this? So I knew at that point, God was not real. So the pain continued, the beatings continued, the nightmares continued. I was in a very dark place in my life at a very early age.

Year after year of being put in the dark closet as a punishment, it just became a familiar place for me. It had gotten to the point when I got yelled at for whatever reason, I just got up and went to the closet. I was no longer afraid of the fact that sometimes there were roaches that would crawl on me in the closet to the point where all I could do was sit there and wish I were dead. I even remember hoping that the roaches would just eat me up, thinking that would be a way out of this misery. I can remember as if it was yesterday, seeing the look on my sister Debbie's face as tears ran down her eyes, screaming out to our relative, "please don't hurt my sister, please don't hurt her."

There had been many nights when I was sent to bed with nothing to eat and having to wash all of the dishes after everyone else had eaten. I literally remember taking my finger and licking what was left on someone else's plate because I was so hungry. My sister would hide food in her clothes when I was done cleaning up, and she would hand me pieces of food off of her plate. If ever there was a dirty dish that I had missed cleaning, I had to take everything out of the cabinets and start all over again. Sometimes it took me until dawn to finish washing all of those dishes, and still, I had to make sure I was up and ready for school the next morning.

Many nights I just wondered how I could make it through another day. I know how, because I have my sister Debbie right there by my side, always telling me that everything would be alright. My sister was not just my sister; she became my mother, best friend, teacher, and much more. Sometimes I felt so sad inside because I've always felt that because of me, she did not have such a good childhood. My sister was always there to protect me. She combed my hair every morning for school; she held my hand, crossing the streets. She made sure I had lunch money even if she gave me hers. My sister would make sure I had clean clothes for school, and she was always right there when the bell rang to walk me home. I felt as though I robbed my sister from enjoying her life and took away her childhood.

I was in my last year of elementary school, and Debbie was starting Jr. High School and I just didn't know what I was going to do now that she was going to another school, but I did begin to meet new friends. Needless to say, I never got to have a relationship with any of them outside of school because my relative seldom let me go anywhere, sometimes not even outside to play. Once I got to Jr. High School, I started running track, and I was really good at it. But when I think about it, running allowed me to escape from reality, and every time I ran, I would run like I was running for my life. I had gotten so good that the coach told me with practice and guidance, he could take me all the way to the Olympics.

I think that was the first time I literally felt joy in a very long time. I worked really hard and won many medals and trophies. But when my relative realized how much I enjoyed running, she took me off of the track team and put me on the tennis team. I hated it so much, but if I knew back then what I know now, I could've been a tennis superstar. While I was playing tennis, I made it to the tournaments and out of 45 people, I came in 5th place. Not so bad for a beginner. But I stopped going to practice just because it was something she wanted me to do and not what I wanted to do.

I tried out for the cheerleading team and got picked, but my relative told me that I could not be a cheerleader. I got really good grades in school, well I think that was because of the fear of what would happen to me if I didn't. I realized she was right when she said I would never amount to anything because I really never got to experience doing anything long enough to realize my full potential. I tried really hard to think about the good times I had when I lived in Detroit, Michigan, how I would wake up on Saturdays so excited because I knew my mom or dad was going to take me roller skating or to the park or go get ice cream.

Well, trying to think of all the good times I had back home only made me miss my mom more, so the depression set right back in. Thinking about being back in Michigan reminded me of that moment when my oldest sister woke Debbie and me up and said, "Mommy is not coming home from the hospital." My oldest sister was crying so hard, and I couldn't seem to get that thought out of my head. At that moment, I could not fathom the thought that I would never see my mother again. Now I'm feeling rage, thinking to myself, how could my mom leave us like this?

Years and years passed by, and I just couldn't stop being mad at my mom. I do remember my mom always taking my sisters and me to church on Sundays, but we were very young, and when my mom got sick, I would always hear her praying to God. And to top it off, I was mad at God. Don't let me forget how mad I was at my dad too, because when she died, I felt like he just gave up on us and gave us away. So at this point, I was just mad at everything and everybody.

My sister, Debbie, was a year and a half older than me. My 16th birthday was coming up, and I realized it's time to start thinking about a plan for my sister and me to run away. Before I gave it a second thought, I had grabbed a small bag of clothes and told my sister, "Let's go."She looked at me as if I had lost my mind. She told me she did not want to leave because she was afraid. So I looked back at her with tears in my eyes and said goodbye. I ran out of the door, leaving my sister behind. I ran as fast as I could. Not having a clue where I was going, but I just kept running.

I found myself in a phone booth at some corner store and just sat on the floor of the phone booth, thinking, "Okay, what's next?"As I sat on that dirty ground in that phone booth, the sun began to set, and I was becoming afraid and famished, not knowing what to do next. Mind you; I didn't have a nickel to my name. I began to think about my sister, thinking to myself now that I'm gone what will happen to her. What was I really thinking was I being selfish only thinking about myself? I was hoping that my relative would not turn her anger towards Debbie and began treating her the way that I was being treated. Deep down inside, I knew that that was furthest from the truth; after all, everybody in the family knew how sweet and kind my sister was.

Well, I don't think I was in that phone booth very long, but it sure seemed like hours and hours and hours went by. A lady opened the phone booth door, and to her surprise, there I was sitting on the ground, I'm sure I had to have startled her. She asked me if I was lost. I said, "No, ma'am, I'm not lost;" I'm just waiting for a friend. She said, "Well, may I use the phone?" So I grabbed my bag of clothes and stepped outside of the phone booth while she made her call. Little did I know, the lady had called the police and when the police showed up, they asked me a bunch of questions, and then they took me back home. I knew I was in big trouble, but I was too scared to tell the police what was really going on because I figured me and my sister would get put in some foster care or orphanage and it could be even worse than where I was, or better yet, they may split my sister and me up, so I kept my mouth shut.

Needless to say, I got beaten really badly and sent to my room where my relative told me I had to sit on the floor for the rest of the night. She told me it's a privilege to sleep in the bed, and that I didn't deserve to sleep there in the first place. Well, years have gone by, and I am turning 18 years old, and living here just became the norm, pretty much something that I had adjusted to. My dad was sending money for us once a month and he would call and check on us from time to time, and the last time we talked, he must have really heard the distress in my voice because a few months later, he and my grandmother came to Florida and took my sister and me back to Detroit, Michigan.

I realized that my dad really did love us, and he actually sent us to live in Florida because that was my mother's dying wish. But through all that I endured as a child, what didn't kill me only made me stronger. I had come to understand at this point that my relatives took my sister and me in, and they were only doing the best they could. After all, they added two additional children into their home, and I can only think, maybe being there, we were the ones that disrupted their happy home. I am not excusing the fact that I was verbally and physically abused when I was living there. I have learned through this whole ordeal to just keep pushing. There was no way that I could forget my life as a child, but I needed to learn to forgive. I'm still a work in progress.

Chapter 2

There's No Place like Home

We are finally back home in Michigan. This was the happiest moment of my life. My sister and I got to sleep back in our own beds. You talk about a sigh of relief. I was screaming from the rooftop. My sister got a job, and I finished high school, well I almost finished high school. So here's what happened!!! I met this guy on my way home from school one day, and he was so tall and charming with this really deep voice. He pulled over in his car and got out and starts telling me all the things a young girl loves to hear. He asked me if I wanted a ride home from school and I told him that I was fine with walking.

Guess what he did? He said, "Well, I will walk with you." I was thinking to myself, WOW! Because I won't take a ride with him, he's going to walk with me? Okay, so now he's really winning me over. Mind you, I was not allowed to talk to guys when I lived in Florida, so this was something new and exciting to me. I was still a virgin and very naïve, so I believed anything and everything he said to me. Moreover, I was fascinated with the fact that he would meet me after school every day and kept asking me could he give me a ride home.

So one particular day, I said yes. As you would expect, we didn't go straight home, and 4 weeks later, I found out I was pregnant. You see, back in my day, you couldn't go to school if you were pregnant, so I hid it from everyone as long as I could. I was in the 12th grade, and I had 8 months to graduation, and it had gotten out that I was having a baby, so I was told the only way I could graduate was that I would have to go to a school for pregnant women. That was how things were back in the day.

The school called my dad and told him that I could no longer attend school. So, he was well aware that I was pregnant, and the school counselor explained to him the alternatives. Well, since the school had already told my dad, I figured what the heck, let me just go home and face the music. When I got home, I wasn't expecting what I found out. He had set all of my clothes packed in boxes on the front porch and told me I was not bringing a baby in his house and that I had to find somewhere else to live. Well, here we go again. He's just throwing me away just like before, but not only is he throwing me away, he's throwing away his grandchild.

I called my so-called boyfriend, the father of my baby, and told him that I was pregnant and some woman answered the phone and wanted to know who I was. I said, "I'm his girlfriend," she asked me, "How can you be his girlfriend?" I was like, "What?"

At that moment, she clearly let me know that she was his wife and they had been married for 5 years. She told me to hold on and she would go get him so that he can tell me himself. So when he got on the phone, I asked him if the woman's claim was true. "Is that your wife?" He said yes, as if it was no big deal to him. I just hung up the phone, and tears were falling like a waterfall. I couldn't believe what was happening right at that moment. I loved him so much, he took my virginity, and he is the father of my son.

I had nowhere to go, so I called my cousin that I had lived with in Florida, and she told me that she had joined the military. I told her my situation and explained to her everything that had happened. At the time, she was stationed in Washington, DC, and said that it would be okay for me to come live with her. Immediately, she went straight to the bus station and paid for my ticket to come to Washington, DC. So me and my big belly got on the bus and headed to DC.

She was a blessing and my angel in disguise. Once I arrived at her house, she welcomed me with open arms and told me not to worry about anything because she would take care of me until I have my baby. So, I was showing, walking around looking like I swallowed a basketball, but I was really happy. Once I got settled in at her house, I went back to complete school so that I could be sure to become a high school graduate. My cousin was a nurse in the military, so she knew just what to do. She kept telling me that I was about to have my baby really soon and that I will have my baby before my due date.

My baby was due December 28, but lo and behold, I went into labor on December 25. I was in labor for 14 hours, and my baby just missed being a Christmas baby. I had a beautiful baby boy 6lbs 7oz, and he was the joy of my life and the most beautiful baby ever. My cousin taught me everything about being a mother and not just that, she taught me how to be a lady. My cousin became my best friend. Well, until I met the man of my dreams. He too was in the military, and around the time I met him, my son was only one month old. He immediately became so attached to my baby, and in a very short time, he was treating him like he was his very own son, and within 6 months, he asked me to marry him.

Chapter 3

Best Friends for Life

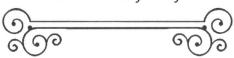

I somehow could not believe life could be this good. I ran off to the justice of the peace and walked out a married woman. I had never met such a kind and loving man as he was. This man gave my son and me the whole world. He got a house on the military base and then bought me a car. This was big to me because I had never had anyone treat my son and me the way he did.

My husband and I were heading to the swimming pool one sunny Saturday afternoon, and he looked over at me and said, "Kim, could you please do me a favor," I said, "Anything for you love." Then he said, "Can you please stop calling him your son and call him our son?" My heart melted. This was truly my best friend for life. Some may have called it puppy love or say we were just crushing because I was only 19, and he was 20. But we knew for whatever reason; we were meant to be together.

Life was so beautiful, and my son loved him so much that they went everywhere together, and yes, he called him daddy, after all, that was the only man he knew. My son's first words were not mommy; they were daddy. They had such a bond that when I would leave the house and say, "Mommy will be right back," he would just wave. But when his dad would leave out of the door, that boy would scream at the top of his lungs. Well, I had become a military wife, but it wasn't long before I found a job because I was never the type to just stay home all day.

Once I begin working, I met so many nice people. I had become really good friends with my next-door neighbor. She was the first one I met when we moved on to the military base. She showed me where the commissary was (a grocery store), took me to the military dances, and I was living my best life.

One thing everyone probably knows about the military is that you could always get stationed in a completely different state before you even realize it. So my husband got orders to move to San Francisco, California, and I had to say goodbye to all my friends that I had made in the 5 years we were stationed in Washington, DC. So we got everything packed up, and the military moved the bulk of our things and the rest. We loaded up in the U-Haul and hit the highway on that long drive to sunny California. After almost 42 hours of driving, we made it, but we did take a few overnight stays at hotels to rest up.

We made it to sunny California, and it was so beautiful in this city. I really wanted to say that I had smiled so much that my cheeks were hurting. As tired as I was, I still wanted to go to the beach especially since I had already heard so much about the beaches there. But once we unloaded that U-Haul truck, it was pretty much a rap. All I could think about was getting me, my husband, and our son something to eat. Then we went off to bed.

The next morning, I was ready to hit the ground running, looking for a job, getting our son in school, and making a life with my husband in a whole different state. I began working for the electric company there in San Francisco and moved up the ranks pretty quickly, where I became a supervisor.

I think this is what most people would call just living life. Things couldn't get any better. I began going out for drinks with people in the company, although I was never much of a drinker, I just enjoyed the company. There was a co-worker that I had become really close to only to find out that her husband was also in the military, and they stayed not that far from us. So she and I became such good friends that we found ourselves doing everything together.

I have always been a fashionista, but she had me beat. I always would admire her class and how she dressed and how she had such a pleasant and outgoing personality. Not to mention, she always had a lot of money. So by now she and I had become such good friends that I felt comfortable enough to ask her how she was able to get such expensive clothes and nice cars and always has a pocket full of money. She told me she would tell me soon enough, so now this really made me curious to the point where I was literally begging her to tell me.

She told me that she had a part-time job. I asked her if she was doing something illegal. She looked at me, laughed, and she said, "Of course not," then I told her that wherever she was working, I'm all in. Later on, I asked her if they were still hiring wherever she was working to make that kind of money. She said, "Ask your husband if you can go with me, and I will introduce you to my supervisor." My husband said it was okay for me to go with her, so I was dressed and ready to find out where she was making all this money. She told me she worked in a club, so when I walked into the club, it was a strip club, but it didn't surprise me or anything. But when we walked into the club, everybody knew her and was not calling her by the name I knew her as. So the antennas went up as well as the curiosity.

I figured she was working as a waitress or bartender and was making really good tips. But, that was not the case at all. She told me to give her a second that she would be right back. Then, she came out on that stage, and my eyes got so big. All I was thinking was, "No, that's not the same person I know in the day time." When I saw all that money that those men were throwing at her, I could not believe it.

So when we left the club, I was so mesmerized. I asked her to tell me what I need to do to dance like that. Well, she got me the job, and I had to lie and tell my husband I was a waitress at a bar, and the rest is history. After working at this club for a few months, there were so many of the women saying you can dance better if you do cocaine. I asked my friend did she do it, and she said, "Yes, I do it from time to time." So I said why not, and she would let me snort some of her drugs and, I danced to the point of no return.

I thought I was on top of the world. I began doing more and more cocaine. I started lying more and more to my husband. My whole attitude changed, but I told myself, "I got this under control."I thought with all of the money I was making, and the new things I was always buying him and our son that he would just overlook the fact that I was not that sweet, kind, and caring woman he married. That's the lies the enemy tells us. I started looking at my friend as my role model; she became my idol. I found myself acting like her, talking like her, even walking like her.

My friend introduced me to a woman that told me that if I smoked cocaine, I would be even better at stripping than I already was. So, of course, I was game. I was making so much money, and thought to myself, "If I smoke cocaine, I could make even more money." I was taught how to cook cocaine, which was called freebasing back in the day, but today it's called crack, and from the moment I began smoking crack, my life completely changed. I lost my real job because I was caught many times at my desk, sleeping. After an all-night binge of smoking crack, all the money I made at the strip club went straight to the drug dealer that was always nearby, yes, right there at the club. So I didn't have to go far to get it.

Chapter 4

Drugs Got the Best of Me

I began leaving my son with my husband all the time. I was not even coming home for some days at a time. I just stopped caring about everything and everybody. Well, except for the drugs. At this point, my husband became fully aware that I was on drugs, and he also knew I was a stripper. He tried everything he could to get me help, but I was just not interested.

I got to the point where I was so strung out that while my son was in elementary school, I forgot to pick him up, and by the time I finally remembered and arrived at the school, he was nowhere to be found. For God sake, he was only 6 years old. I searched up and down the streets crying and screaming his name, asking everybody that I saw if they had seen my kid. I knew that it had to be a God because I saw his little body running towards me as he was crying, calling "Mommy."

He jumped in my arms, saying, "Mommy, I'm so sorry I couldn't find you, so I started walking, and I got lost."He said, "Remember, mommy, you told me that I was a big boy." All I could do with tears streaming down my face was to hold him in my arms. Even after such a tragic event, once we got back to where we were living, I fixed him a sandwich, turned cartoons on for him, and went back in the basement, and I continued to get high.

Where did the time go? Five years had gone by, and my son is now 11. I found myself doing whatever it took to get high. My husband told me enough is enough, and if I did not get help, he would take our son and leave. I couldn't believe what came out of his mouth. But why would I? By this time, I'm a full-blown crack addict, and of course, my thinking was very distorted. I've turned into someone I didn't recognize anymore. We began arguing all the time and our marriage as we had known it went from great to good, from bad to worst. At this point, I could care less about whether or not my husband knew I was a stripper. Evidently, he was not that naïve to not have known.

So after a long night of getting high I came home to a note on the fridge that said, "I took our son to your cousin's house, and I am leaving you." So with such devastation, that he really did what he said he was going to do, the first thing that came to my mind was to get high. I realized that I hated dealing with my feelings, and all I wanted to do was to run and use drugs just so that I wouldn't feel anymore. I was just wondering how he could do this to me because everything was always about me once I had those drugs in me.

I thought we took a vow for better or worse. I was so selfish and self-centered, I didn't even think, let me call to see where my husband is or let me call and check on my son. I went on a week binge not calling to check to see if my son was alright, I didn't even go back to the house. All I did was go from dope house to dope house selling my body just to get one more high.

After I had exhausted all avenues of getting any more drugs, I decided to call my cousin, not so much to check to see how my son was doing but to call and ask for some money. She said she was so worried about me because I hadn't even called to check on my son. She wanted to know if I was okay. I told her I was fine and would be coming to get my son on the weekend.

Well, after being in the streets every day, going to get my son was not an option. I stayed here and there as long as I could until I came back from getting high to a big yellow eviction notice on the door, which was padlocked. I couldn't even go in and get any of our belongings, not that there was even much left in the house because I had pretty much sold everything. I eventually found myself sleeping in my car. I can't say I lost anything, so I will be honest and say I sold many things.

I pawned my car, knowing I would never get it back. I also pawned my wedding ring, which I knew I would never get back. I sold everything in my house that was not nailed down, everything from the microwave to the plates and glasses in my cabinet. I was sleeping from pillar to post, wondering when the day would come that they would come and repossess the car that I had already pawned to the drug dealer.

I called my cousin to inform her that I had gotten evicted and I just didn't know what to do about my son. She told me there's no way that she would let me get him in the condition I was in. Well, my cousin kept my son for a whole year. And honestly, I couldn't believe how a year quickly went by. I was still on the streets getting high, I missed my son's birthday, I missed his Christmas, and my car finally had gotten repossessed. I was homeless, hopeless, and I don't even have my son.

After several years of non-stop getting high, my life was in shambles. I decided it's time for me to get my life together. I was determined to stop using drugs cold turkey. Of course, it was not that easy. I called my dad and begged him to please let me and my son come back to Michigan. He had no clue what a mess I had made of my life. But he did send a ticket to the bus station for my son and me to come back to Michigan.

I got a ride to my cousin's house and told her that my son and I were going back to Michigan. She looked at how bad I looked, and I could see the hurt and pain in her eyes. She said, "Well, Kim, you can go ahead, but please let your son stay here with me until you get yourself together." All she was doing was trying to help me, and I found myself going off on her saying you're just trying to take my son, and you can't have him. I promised her that once I got back to Michigan, I would get myself together and make her proud.

So we went off to Michigan. I fixed myself up so that no one back home would even be the wiser. I came back to Michigan, and I hit the ground running. I always knew I was pretty smart because from kindergarten to the 12th grade; I always got all A's and B's. So, my father told me to go and take the test for the city and see if I can get a job working for the City of Detroit because they were hiring. So that's just what I did. The test was a 2-hour test, but I completed the test in 50 minutes.

I was called to come and work for the city because they told me that I had passed the test with a 98% score. My sister took me shopping to get some suits for work and all while I'm getting ready to start working for the city, all I could think about was getting high. I've got to get this thought out of my mind. This was not an easy task, but I knew in my heart that I never wanted to go down that road again. So now I'm officially working for the city of Detroit, and I couldn't be happier. I had to work 2 weeks in a row before I could get my check, and it didn't even matter to me. Just knowing that I'm getting my life back on track and providing for my son was the most important thing.

Well, now a whole year into working for the city, and I got a big surprise. I was told that I was going to be promoted to a supervisor. I couldn't wait to get home to tell everybody the good news. I got my first check with my promotion, and the drugs began calling me louder and louder. My dad was retired, so he would let me use his car to go to work, but this particular day, I got in the car to go to work and never made it. I found myself in a drug-infested area, asking where I could get some crack. I didn't go home for a few days, and I had my family worried sick about me. But in my mind, I thought who cares. I felt like I was back doing what I was familiar doing.

See, all I could think about was how I enjoyed the high, and not once did I think about where the drugs took me when I lived in California, how I lost everything including my son, but by this time, I had already opened Pandora's Box. My father kicked me out once again, and my son and I packed up and moved in with my sister. My sister became my enabler because she knew I was getting high, but she'd rather give me money than to see me out in the streets doing everything to get high. She took good care of my son, so I never had to worry about him. This was my pass to get cracked out over and over again.

While I was on the streets, I met this guy that told me I was too pretty to be out here on the streets like this, and if I were his woman, I wouldn't be doing what I was doing. So me being me, I said what the heck, so I grabbed my son once again and packed up our few things and moved in with him. He really was a nice guy with a good job, and for the life of me, I couldn't see what he saw in me. He took good care of my son, fed us, bought us clothes, took my son to school, and this was just too good to be true. But it was real; this was a good guy who generally cared. He already knew that I used drugs, so that was no secret, but he told me the only conditions he had was that I kept the house clean, make sure dinner was ready when he came home from work and he said he better not ever catch me getting high in front of my son.

That was easy enough. I got this. If he were ever home, he would only allow me to get high in the bathroom, and he told me to lock the door so that my son would not walk in on me. Okay, easy enough. So I did everything he asked me until one day I asked him to do me a favor. I said, "Why don't you come try getting high with me?" What in the world was I thinking? I was so freaking selfish. I was only thinking about me, myself, and, I. He was really a good, loving, and caring guy. Still, I kept pressuring him to get high because I was thinking to myself, "He has a really good job, and if he gets high with me, instead of him giving me a few dollars here and there, we can just spend all of his money together."

He gave in and tried it with me one day. Months went by, he was still working, but he began to drink to come down from the high. I've created a monster. It didn't take long for the arguing and the fighting to begin. Dang! I really didn't think this thing through. He started drinking more and more, and now he's staying out all night going on binges. I asked myself, "What have I done?"

When he would come in from getting drunk and high, all he seemed to want to do was fight. Needless to say, the lights, heat, and water got cut off. Could my heart have been so cold to bring someone into the world I hated being in myself? He spiraled out of control way quicker than I imagined. I started feeling awful for even introducing him to such a terrible life of drugs.

But there's something that I do need to mention. I did run into him some years later, and he had gotten himself together. He was no longer drinking or smoking crack. He actually told me that he was doing really well. Of course, he really did look great. He had gotten married and had a son. But for my son and me, we were back on the streets because I never did stop using. Now my son and I were homeless; we were living in drug houses, lying on people's floors living wherever we could. I would go up to the gas stations begging for change just to be able to get my son a bag of chips and juice for a meal.

Well, it wasn't long before I had met another guy; actually, he was one of my regulars. He told me that he was catching feelings for me, and he really wants to help my son and me. Before I knew it, he asked if we wanted to move in with him. Because this guy was one of my regulars, he knew quite a bit about me because we talked all of the time. He told me about his wife passing and that he had four teenage boys that lived with him. It wasn't like I was going to turn him down; after all, my son and I had nowhere else to stay. So I gathered up our stuff again, and we moved in with him.

My son and his four sons seemed to get along really well. They were all going to the same school together. The guy that moved us in said I was now his girlfriend, so I guess he was my boyfriend. Things really worked out great for a while because there were no secrets between us; he had known quite a bit about me from all of our talks. He supplied my drugs for me so that I wouldn't have to go out and trick to get them.

I thought within myself, "Why do I keep picking these same kinds of men? Is my self-esteem that low that I just continue to allow these men to beat on me? I guess I'm really worthless." I was almost sure that because I use drugs, I pretty much deserve whatever happens to me. Although these things may not be true, that was how I felt.

It was not long before this man began to beat me black and blue. My son had started living from pillow to post himself, so he was not there to see how this man was beating me. I thank God that he was not there because we all know that no son will allow a man to put his hands on his mother. My son may have ended up dead or in jail if he was still at that house with me.

When this man would black my eyes and my son would come over to check on me, the man would tell him I was not home that I was out in the streets somewhere. When all along, he told me I better not say anything or even think about screaming. It had gotten so bad living there that before he left for work, he would handcuff me to the bed with a bottle of water, a sandwich, and a bucket to use the bathroom. He would not even allow me to be handcuffed on the bed; he would handcuff me at the bottom rail of the bed where I was on the floor.

This really was something like you would see on TV. When he would come home for lunch, I would beg him to please let me go, and I promised I wouldn't run away if he just unhandcuffed me. I learned never to ask that question again because he kicked me in the stomach and told me never to ask him that question ever again.

I pretty much became his sex slave, and not only that, he would let his sons have their way with me. I was living in hell. You know people always say when you're in an abusive relationship, why don't you just leave. But for those of you that have never been there, let me explain to you, it's not that easy. The threats and fear have you so paralyzed that you'll be forced to make up your mind that the only way out is death.

One of his sons felt so bad for me that he told me that he had a key to the handcuffs, and if he let me go, I should take the chance to run. So while his dad was at work, he let me go. I took off running out of that house like it was on fire. I went straight to the police station, and because I had so many bruises, they went to his house to arrest him. When I heard that he was in jail, it was such a relief, but I let my guards down. I later realized he didn't stay there for long; they only kept him overnight, then they released him.

Before I knew it, he came looking for me with a vengeance. People in the neighborhood told me he was out looking for me, and I had never been so afraid. He paid a crack head to tell him where I was, and this man came to this house where I was hiding out and threw a brick through the window, telling me I had better come out, or he was going to burn the house down. The person that was allowing me to hide out said that man is crazy, and I had to get out of his house. So I had to face the music.

He dragged me by my hair all the way back to his house down the middle of the street, and there were people saying, "Hey, leave her alone," but no one stopped him or even stopped to help me. So once we got back to his house, he threw me in the basement, and that's where he left me for days with no food or water. After being in that basement for about 2 weeks, the same son that let me go the first time came to the basement and said, "I cannot take this anymore. Kim, if I let you go, you've got to get out of the neighborhood."

So this time, I went back to the police station and told them what he had done to me once they had released him. I was crying so hard that they told me if I press charges, they can keep him longer. Then, I pressed charges, and they locked him up for 30 days, during which I was able to go to a battered women's shelter. The shelter I went to only allowed me to stay for 3 days, so after the 3 days, I was back at square one.

While I'm being very transparent and sharing what the drugs did to me and what I did to get the drugs, I know I need to continue sharing my story and as painful as it is and how I may be judged or looked at, I have to continue to share the truth so that I can be set free.

THE PAIN I CAUSED MY SON

You can only imagine what I had subjected my son to. One thing that I made sure of no matter how high I got or where it was, I made sure my son was in my eyesight. I was so afraid that if I took my eye off him that someone in that drug house would try to molest him, and I would never allow that. If I got up to use the bathroom, the first thing I would ask my son was that "Did anybody touch you, did anybody say anything to you." I would ask my son that so much that if he were ever out of my eyesight for a second, he would say, "Mom, nobody touched me" because he knew I was going to ask. Could you imagine your child having to live like that for just a minute?

My son, now 16 years old, figured enough is enough. He struck out on his own. He met a young lady and moved in with her and her parents. At such an early age, he ended up having a baby, my grandson. Of course, I didn't get to see him born, nor did I even go see him after he was born because the drugs were so much more important. Then they broke up, and he ended up moving with another girl who also got pregnant, another grandson, then he moved back with the first girl and, yes, yet another grandson. My son had no structure because I was never with him long enough to teach him, and he was just looking to be loved.

His life was basically out of control. What do you expect? So was his mother's life, and I was the only role model he had. He made it to the 12th grade, but he wanted to work and try to help take care of his kids, so he dropped out of school. My son had absolutely no direction in life and began hanging around the wrong crowd, where he started drinking. I knew that he began drinking to numb the pain of his mom being out on the streets, and I'm sure it was a constant worry for him. It became all too familiar running from our pain, and that's where the drugs and alcohol came in to play to numb the pain. But I thank God to this day that he did not take the same path I did, getting hooked on drugs.

He remained friends with the sons of the man that had abused me, and one of the sons was stealing cars and breaking into houses, and I heard about it in the streets. I began asking around if anybody had seen my son because I knew this was not the road I wanted my son to go down. I finally found out where he was living, and we had a long talk. I may have been a crack head, but I'm still a mother. He promised me that he was not doing what his friend was doing because he didn't want to die. He knew that the things his friend was doing are criminal, that it would be a matter of time he would either get killed or go to jail.

Well, not long afterwards, I had gotten word that my son was in the hospital. I was told he was involved in a fatal accident while joy riding in a car stolen by his friend. I got to the hospital and found my son sitting in the waiting room, with his head bandaged and cuts on his face, but he was okay. I had never seen him cry as hard as he was crying. He said, "Mom, we hit a tree, and my friend went through the windshield, and he is dead. All I could do was drop my head and say thank God it was not you. Yes, my thinking was very distorted. It wasn't that I didn't care about this young man, but all I could think was he was still the son of a man that brutally beat me.

Soon after, the police came and arrested my son because they could not charge his friend with stealing, so they charged my son. He was only 16 years old, but they still charged him and sent him to boot camp, and this caused him to have a felony on his record "receiving stolen property, "and my son still has that charge on his record to this day. Of course, this has made it impossible for him to get a good job. And did I even mention that all he ever talked about was that he wanted to become a Veterinarian?

He loved animals so much, and I was not there for him to help him follow his dream. He had totally given up, and once he got out of boot camp, he began drinking even more. He told me that it's really hard for him to walk down the streets and people yelling out to him, "I just saw your crack head momma or your momma was just in an alley turning a trick." My son had so many fights because guys would tease him about his mother being a crack head. I decided it was best for me to start hanging out in a different neighborhood because I didn't want someone to hurt my son over me.

Yes, that was my delusional thinking again. What I should have been thinking was, "It's time for me to stop using drugs." But once I changed neighborhoods, I looked at it as being a blessing in disguise because there was an abandoned apartment building that I ended up making it my home. I looked in garbage cans or wherever I could to find some old clothes or whatever so that I could make something to sleep on. I made it work. I lived in this abandoned building for almost a year. I fed myself by eating out of the garbage; I remember standing at the gas station begging for money, and I even offered to pump people's gas.

There was a guy sitting in his car, and I saw him take a bite out of a sandwich and then throw it in the garbage. I couldn't wait until he pulled off so that I could run and get that sandwich. I was the type of drug addict that was too scared to rob or steal, so I either turned tricks, ask the gas station owner if I could clean up the gas station, or collect bottles. As I said earlier, I was never too proud to beg for money to get my drugs.

With all of the things I've seen and done when I was out in the streets getting high, I was totally surprised I hadn't lost my mind. Like I said, I was never tempted to steal for fear of getting caught. But I was a good lookout girl. There was this guy I frequently got high with, and he told me about this warehouse that has computers in it, and if I keep an eye out for him, he would give me $25. Now you know that was a lot of money to me, so I told him sure but I was not going inside that place.

I was sitting in his van, keeping an eye out, and all I could hear was him screaming my name as he ran out of the doors on fire. And to this day, I don't know what happened when he was in that warehouse, but I remembered jumping out of that van and running down that street as fast as I could. I still cannot get that image out of my head because I still have nightmares watching him burn alive. But did that scare me enough to stop getting high? That would be a "No." Although it shook me up pretty good, as soon as I got back on the block, it was like life goes on.

The scariest thing I had seen was when everybody on the block went running down the street, and I wanted to see what was happening for myself. So I ran right along with everybody else only to see someone I knew shot in the head and thrown in the dumpster. She was pronounced dead, and the coroners had come to pick up her body. Two weeks later, she was walking down the street talking about where are the drugs at? Everybody was looking at her as if we saw a ghost. I literally saw the bullet in her head, and her body being deposited in a body bag. But every time she came around, it was the most eerie feeling you could imagine.

At this point, I knew I was in hell on earth. It was like something out of a horror movie. She still looked like the same person, but her skin was very pale, and her eyes were like there were no pupils just solid black, and there was something about her voice that was just different. If I had never believed in the devil before, she made a believer out of me. Her demeanor was so evil that the drug dealers would not let her in the drug houses. I always looked at myself as the walking dead, but I honestly believe that she was the walking dead.

I headed back to my "abandominium," aka my abandoned apartment building, and decided to get some sleep. I was actually happy knowing that I no longer had to look for somewhere to lay my head at night to the point where I would say I'm going home.

As I woke up in the morning, brushed my teeth, yes, there was running water but no hot water. So all I could do was wash up with cold water, I headed out on a mission with nothing but drugs on my mind. I didn't even get to the end of the block where I was heading to stand on my corner to pick up a trick, and a man stopped me and asked me if I want to get high. Is he kidding right now, of course, I want to get high.

So as we began walking up the street, another man grabbed me from behind and lassoed a belt around my neck and pulled as hard as he could to the point that I couldn't even scream. It was a setup. I remember kicking and trying to scream when they threw me in a van. One of the guys was trying to stop me from fighting, so he just kept punching me in my face and my chest until I blacked out. They had taken me to someplace, but I had no clue where they had taken me because, for the most part, I was unconscious.

As they began to rape me and beat me and rape me over and over again, one of the guys picked up a 2x4 and hit me across my back. I'm not sure what the sharp object was, but one of the guys slit my arm open, and blood was everywhere. One of the guys had split my head open. When that guy hit me in my stomach, it took my breath away to the point where I used the bathroom on myself, and I heard that when you are dying, you release your bodily fluids, so I knew this was the end of my life.

The last thing on my mind before I blacked out was my son. I remember thinking to myself as if he was there, saying son I'm so sorry. At this point, I guess they figured they had killed me, so that took my lifeless body and threw me in an alley. When I woke up, I was lying in a hospital bed, but I have no clue how I got there. I woke up in so much pain. Mind you, the keyword here is that I woke up!!! I honestly knew at this point that there has got to be a God.

I remember calling out to the nurse telling her I was hurting really bad and that I needed something for the pain. She told me I had been seriously beaten, and she really didn't think that I would make it through the night. She asked me if I knew my name and if I knew where I was. My face was swollen beyond recognition because my forehead had been busted open, and I had to get 8 stitches. I had two black eyes and 32 stitches in my arm and a blood clot in my thigh. She told me I had been in the hospital for 4 days and my wristband said, Jane Doe. I didn't have any identification on me, much less insurance.

So on the 7th day, although I was still in extreme pain, they released me from the hospital. I walked all the way back from Henry Ford hospital back to Linwood, where I was staying in that abandoned building. During the entire walk back to where I was living, I was constantly looking over my shoulder because I was afraid those guys would see me and finish me off. I could not tell you what they looked like, what they were wearing, or even the maker of the van they were driving. The experience was so horrific to the point where I just didn't want to remember. Once I made it back home, I didn't go back outside for 2 days, but the drugs were calling my name, and even more so, I needed to eat something.

After what just happened, how could I still be thinking about getting high? You may hear many people that have never had a drug addiction say just stop using. But do you even understand why I can't just stop using drugs at this point after so many years? Having a drug addiction is a monster. It is a stronghold that you can't just shake off. I have heard people that have been on drugs say they just woke up one morning and said I'm never using drugs again, but I was not one of those exceptional people. I cannot even count how many times I told myself this is the last time I will use drugs. I cannot count how many times I threw the pipe and all of my paraphernalia in the trash only to go back and get it out of the trash.

After a few days of being released from the hospital, I was still really sore, and I still had two black eyes. Even though they had lightened up a bit, I still had what looked like blood in my eyes, but I just couldn't lie there any longer. I told myself I was going to do something different this time.

There was a church on the corner, so I said if I stand in front of this church and pick up a trick, then I will be safe. Wow!!! I can't even believe I thought like that. It was something about standing in front of that church that made me feel safe. The first day back on the corner, in front of that church, a car pulled up and asked me what I would do for $20. I said, "What do you want me to do?" He got out of the car and showed me his badge and said I was under arrest for soliciting. He handcuffed me and put me in the back of his car. Mind you; I was sitting right in front of the church, where I said I felt safe.

The police officer never started to drive off, and he just looked back at me in that back seat crying my eyes out, and he said, "What happened to you?" You look like you've been through hell. Don't forget I had stitches in my forehead and two black eyes. He said, "Look, I'm going to let you go, but you need to get some help because if you don't, you're going to die out here in these streets." He told me that I could not even imagine how many times he had been called to a scene where a prostitute had been murdered. There was a sigh of relief. And I promised him I would get help.

As I walked back down the street going to where I lived, I looked back at that church, and all I could think was WOW!!! I think God just saved me again. As you would expect, shortly afterward, maybe about an hour, I was right back on that corner in front of that church literally praying; please don't let me run back into that officer. I'm sure I was not praying to God, after all, I was a faithful soldier for Satan all these years and facing reality, the things I was on the streets doing, I'm pretty sure I was not a child of God. But I figured after waiting for about an hour; I should be good to go back up to my corner. As I was standing on the corner, guess who pulled up? No, not that police officer, not someone asking me to go get high with them, it was my oldest sister.

Out of all the people in the world, she was definitely not someone I wanted to see. Had it been my sister, Debbie, it would not have been anything out of the norm because she was always doing drive-bys just checking up on me. I wanted to get high so bad, and for the life of me, I couldn't understand what was going on with all of these roadblocks that are preventing me from getting high.

My oldest sister is a no-nonsense type of gal. She called me over to the car and saw how beat up I was, and she just began to cry. She was begging me to come over her house just for one night and take a hot shower and eat a good meal. She told me that she promised she would bring me back the next day. So after all of the things that have happened in one day, I thought maybe this is some kind of sign that I needed to get off of that corner, so I went to my sister's house, took a hot shower, and ate a delicious home-cooked meal. I slept in a comfortable bed, and I thought I was in heaven.

Well, the next morning came, and she got up and fixed me a hot breakfast, and gave me some clean clothes to put on. We got in her car, and I was smiling from ear to ear just thinking about getting back on Linwood so that I could get high. As we were driving back to Detroit, she said my dad was in the hospital, and she wanted to make a quick stop to check on him. She asked me, "Wouldn't I like to see my dad? Since she was driving and I didn't have much of a choice, I agreed. Well, we were driving and driving and driving to the point where I started getting really irritated, so I asked her, "Where are we going?" Actually, I didn't say it like that because while I was in my addiction, I had a real potty mouth, and every other word I used was profanity. She told me that they had to take my dad way out of town because that was the hospital he had to go to.

So after about a 2-hour drive, we pulled up to this winding dirt road. I thought we had gotten lost, but she was listening to Google maps, and it was giving her direction to go the way she was going. So we went down this dirt road for about a good 15 minutes and pulled up in front of this big brown building. Of course, I assumed it was the hospital, but she told me to wait in the car because she wanted to go inside and ask if my dad could have two visitors at one time. My sister came back outside with some lady, my sister reached in the car and popped the trunk and told me to come on.

When I got out of the car, she had packed a suitcase for me, sat it on the curb, jumped in her car, and took off. All I could see was her arm waving out the window saying, "I love you, Kim; this is going to hurt me more than it's going to hurt you." So you could imagine the surprised look on my face. As my sister speed down that dirt road rocks kicking up from her tires, I was throwing rocks at her car, calling her all kinds of names. I was in disbelief. I had no idea where she had dropped me off. But that lady she came outside with was standing there while I was throwing a fit.

The lady told me to calm down and to come inside. I asked her where I was. She said you're at the treatment center. At that point, all hell broke loose. I told that lady I was not staying there, and I wanted to go home. She was crazier than she looked if she thought for one minute I was walking through those doors. She said to me with this really kind voice that I could stay outside as long as I wanted, and I was welcome to come inside when I was ready. I sat there on the steps with my suitcase that my sister had packed crying like a baby.

Some girl came outside and sat next to me. She gave me a big hug and asked me what my name was as if I wanted to talk to somebody. She introduced herself to me and began telling me it's not that bad that I should just give the treatment a try. She finally talked me into coming inside, well actually, we were way out in the woods, the sun was going down, and all those little critters started coming out. I saw skunks, raccoons, chipmunks, bats; I was more scared to stay outside than I was mad. So she and I walked through the doors of the treatment center, and that day July 17, 2003, was the first day of the rest of my life.

Chapter 5

Learning How to Live Again

Now that I have no other choice but to make the best of this situation, all I could think was, "Where do I start? How do I begin?"Being in a treatment center means I will never be able to use drugs again, and I just couldn't seem to grasp the thought of never getting high again after getting high for 16 years of my life. Aren't we creatures of habit? I don't know how to do anything else but to scheme, manipulate, and do drugs. I have already convinced myself that this is going to be a challenge. My mindset went back to my relative, telling me that I was never going to be anything in life anyway.

There was so much structure at this treatment center, definitely something that I was not used to. We had to be up every morning at 6:00am, have our shower and rooms cleaned by 7:00am and be at breakfast at 7:30 am. We had to be at our first Narcotics Anonymous meeting from 8:30am to 10:30 am. We were allowed to take a short nap, then lunch at noon, off to another meeting, then a 1-1 with a therapist. But get this; we had to be in bed by 8:00

pm. I thought I was in shock when I realized that I have to be here for 45 days. This is way too much to even comprehend. But as the days went on, this routine became easier and easier. I began to change my mindset. I said earlier that we are creatures of habit, so why can't I change my bad habits into good habits, getting up doing what I am supposed to do and doing the things I need to do to get better. I know there's got to be a better way of life than using drugs. It was like I started getting butterflies in my stomach when actually, I think it was something that I hadn't felt in forever. It was joy!!!

The longer I stayed in that treatment center, the prouder I became of myself. I began making friends. I became in charge of kitchen duties. I began leading the meetings, and I started realizing some of my potentials. All while I was in that treatment center, I told myself that I had leadership skills, and I realized that my gift was that one day I was going to be a motivational speaker. I started being excited to clean my room, wake up, take a hot shower, and eat three meals a day. But there was one thing we were not allowed to do – we could not fraternize with the men; they were located in another building across the way. We all had meetings together, and although I was there to get clean, that old prostitute behavior was still with me.

I met a guy, and we knew it was against the rules to be seen together, so we started writing each other notes about how we could get together. Well, we made it work and started having sex in the treatment center. Being very careful not to get caught, we would sneak in the woods around midnight. But for some reason, after he and I got together a few times, I began feeling some kind of way. I was pleasingly surprised that my conscience wouldn't let me continue to see him. This program was really working. He had already been in the center for a month, and it was about time for him to be released. He promised that he would wait for me when I got out, and our intentions were to get married once I was released.

A week before my release time, I found out that he had relapsed and overdosed. I was given the option to go straight from treatment to the halfway house, and after hearing what happened to him, I told my therapist, "Yes, I was all in." The halfway house was a 90-day program, and it was pretty much the same as being in a treatment center, but you were allowed to go out as a group to attend meetings only. I knew this was the place I needed to be because I was not quite ready to be in the real world on my own.

Once I got in that halfway house, I began to learn everything I needed to know about staying clean. I studied that basic textbook and the 12 step program as if I was back in school again. At this point, I was 45 days clean and never felt so good. I wanted more of what this program had to offer. After all, I was constantly told that you would only get to benefit from what you put into the program. I noticed my behavior began to change; my way of thinking began to change as well. And this was only the beginning. There was so much more I had to do to recover. I had to learn how to deal with my feelings and emotions; after all, that was the reason I started getting high anyway so that I wouldn't have to feel anything.

Well, it's been 90 days in the halfway house, and I was offered the opportunity to go out on my own or to move forward into a ¾ house. This is a house for women that are not quite ready to enter the world as we know it. This ¾ allows you to maintain the structure and continue to work the program of Narcotics Anonymous. I knew I needed to continue to get all the support that was offered to me, so I decided to move into the ¾ house. There were 2 bunk beds in each room, and the house had 3 rooms upstairs and 3 rooms downstairs, so there were 4 women to each room. Yes, I was still in a place with a bunch of women with a whole lot of different personalities and attitudes.

I continued to make the best of the situation with a positive outlook. I looked at all these women in this one house to help me be a better communicator. I looked at the rules as preparing me, just like when I began working. I also looked at the structure as a way to help me learn how to be organized, and as I applied these lessons to my life daily, it was not so hard after all. In each of these programs, there was always something I could take away from it. From the treatment center to the ½ house to the ¾ house has helped me grow tremendously because I made a conscious decision to keep an open mind and do whatever it took to stay clean and recover.

Sometimes in life, you have to realize you may need extra help, so for me, along with making NA meetings, I began seeing a therapist. The NA meetings helped me to get clean, but going to therapy helped me stay clean. I was able to really learn a lot about myself. While working both of these programs, I felt as if I met me for the first time. I began to understand I no longer have to use drugs to deal with my life, when I'm hurt or when things don't go my way or even when there are things in my life that I don't understand. I've learned how to deal with life on life terms.

This is a wonderful journey, so anyone struggling with the use of drugs, or any addiction should take this road to recovery. Don't be afraid to take back control of your life. Never worry about what people say about you when they see you changing. Just remember you are getting clean for you, not your children, spouse, parents, or friends. You are no good to any of them if you are not strictly doing it for yourself. Things that many take for granted, today I give God thanks for those things. Even when I eat a bag of chips or drink a glass of water, even when taking a hot bath, I give God all the praise and glory. You could never imagine living in a life of despair; only if you've ever walked in my shoes, you would know that those little things were hard to come by.

Since I've been clean, I realize how smart I really am. I was just a person who made bad decisions. But I'm almost sure that every one of us at some time in our lives has made one or two bad decisions. Some can be fixed, while some turn out fatal, but I'm almost sure that no one would wake up in the morning and say to themselves, "Let me see how many bad decisions I can make today."That is why, today, I am very conscious of the decisions I make.

It's never too late

I am a grateful recovering addict, a believer of God, a strong and determined woman. I am the kind of person that will never give up learning and striving to be the best version of me that I can be. I love to learn new things; this is why when I got clean, I went to college for 4 years to become a Court Reporter graduating with a 3.99 GPA. I went to school for 2 years to become a Chaplin, and now I am a first responder Lieutenant Chaplin. I am also a volunteer at the Oakland County Jail, where I have served for 14 years as a minister teaching Bible study as well as conducting NA meetings for the women inmates.

I've volunteered as a Chaplin with a program called "No One Dies Alone" at the Hospice centers. My sister and I started our own cleaning business. Just to let you know that it's never too late and you are never too old to start over. You just have to have a positive mindset and determination. I decided to go back to school at Destiny Christian University, where I received my Bachelor's degree in Theology with a concentration in Counseling at the age of 55, graduating with a 4.27 GPA and was asked to give the graduation speech.

I have traveled to 8 different countries to experience their culture. I have jumped out of an airplane; I've been scuba diving in the Gulf of Mexico. I took lessons to learn to fly a helicopter and much more. What I realize is "Tomorrow is not promised, so why not live for today." I no longer take life for granted, and this is why I smile 98% of the time, like I had mentioned before, I remember the days that I couldn't even wash up. So every single time I get in the tub, I thank God. There were times when I had absolutely nothing to eat, so even when I eat a bag of chips, I thank God. Even when I drink a glass of water, I thank God. It may sound silly to you, but if you were ever without, you would understand.

Chapter 6

Life without Drugs

Days turned into months, and months turned into years. Being clean is the most amazing thing one could ever experience after having a 16-year drug addiction. My entire life has changed, I would be lying if I told you that once I stopped using drugs that my life all of a sudden became peaches and cream because that would be far from the truth. It is a journey and an effort that you have to put forth every single day. Day by day, you will begin to enjoy this new way of living and begin to realize that the old ways were not as enjoyable as you thought they were.

I realize today that God has a calling on my life.

From the death of my mother, at such an early age; I'm still standing.

From a suicide attempt; I'm still standing.

From the horrors of 16-year drug addiction; I'm still standing.

From mental and physical abuse that I've had to endure; I'm still standing.

From the emotional feelings of abandonment; I'm still standing.

From being raped, beaten, stabbed, and left for dead; I'm still standing.

From being homeless, cold, and hungry; I'm still standing.

From eating out of garbage cans, eating off the ground, and begging for change; I'm still standing.

From going to college to receive my degree as a Court Reporter, a deer went through my windshield, and I was in a coma for two days. Not to mention, when the deer came through my windshield, it broke several bones in my hand; therefore I could not type, not only that, I was in my 4th year in school, preparing to graduate in 3 months, having to walk across the stage with a cast on my arm; I'm still standing.

I had to start my life over again when I got clean at the age of 42; I'm still standing.

Never will I give up, no matter what, simply because God never gave up on me, and it's only through His grace and His mercy that I'm still standing.

I may not be where I want to be in life, but I thank God I'm not where I used to be. I'm exactly where God needs me to be.

From time to time, I do have to remind myself that God does things in His timing, not in my timing. By staying mindful of this, it allows me to stay patient and not lose sight that the best is yet to come.

The program of Narcotics Anonymous has made a tremendous difference in my life. I realized that the NA program was instrumental, but I needed some extra help. I began seeking extended help with a therapist who allowed me to not just work on the surface of my addiction; but also allowed me to get to the core of my addiction. The NA program showed me that I am not alone. But the therapist made me realize that I had never been alone. The NA program showed me that we all are in this program to motivate one another. It was the love and care that I received from the other members that helped me to understand that we are all here for the same reason, to learn how to live this new way of life without drugs. Today I am clean from all mind and mood-altering chemicals, and I will never look back.

See there's no stopping me now. I realize that I no longer have to run to drugs to mask the pain or deal with my feelings. Today, I run to God.

Mental health

According to the National Institute of Mental Health, an addiction to drugs or alcohol is a mental illness. It changes normal behaviors and interferes with the ability to work, go to school, and to have a good relationship with friends and or family. I was diagnosed with a mental health issue called depression, which led me to the use of drugs. By admitting and understanding my illness, I was able to heal and be delivered from the mental illness of depression.

Relapsing

Although I stayed clean and never wanted to look back, there are still many that just didn't get clean or were not just ready to stop. You often find yourself thinking about relapsing, and then you begin to believe things such as I can have just one drink, one pill, one crack, one pack of dope, not allowing yourself to remember that one is too many and 1000 is never enough. It's important to think about what you are telling yourself. Take a brief second before you pick up and remind yourself that just for today, I never have to use drugs ever again and believe that.

You have to completely strip yourself of that old way of thinking that you thought worked so that you can do what you know will work, after all, using drugs never worked for anyone. So in order to stay drug-free, ask yourself regularly, "What am I going to do differently?" You can begin by simply surrendering. Be open-minded by taking suggestions from those who are clean and have stayed clean. Get a sponsor or someone that holds you accountable for your actions. Be sure to get someone that is not an enabler (enabler definition: in my own words, it's someone that condones your mess) because that will only hinder your recovery. We are great manipulators, and taking that route, will not help you stay on track. Be willing to learn what the program has to offer, stay clean, recover, and there is a difference. Staying clean means that you have stopped using drugs while recovering means that you began to change your old ways of thinking and acting. It's a must that we learn how to deal with our feelings, emotions, and the reality of life and not picking up that first drink or drug. These simple suggestions will take you a long way in your recovery.

Sometimes it's hard to find that silver lining when you're in such a dark place, but you have got to trust the process.

No matter what your situation or circumstance may be, never give up keep smiling, keep dancing, keep singing, keep shining, and keep believing. Don't stay stuck in "What ifs" or "If only."Take the word "I can't" or "It's too hard" out of your vocabulary. Practice speaking nothing but positivity over your life. Do not allow your past to deter you from reaching your full potential for your future. Use those past situations and circumstances to make yourself stronger. We have many resources out there to help us; that's only a call, a website, or social media away. Understand that addiction is much more than just drugs; there are many types of addictions.

There are more people than you think that are struggling with addictions such as sex, gambling, eating, shopping, lying, stealing, and the list goes on and on. But anyone, no matter your race, creed, age, color, religion, or non-religion, can find a new way to live without that addiction. Work the 12-step program, and wherever the word drugs are in that book, replace it with whatever your addiction is. It works if you give it a chance to work for you.

Don't be surprised when those using thoughts come or those using dreams come, or people that you used to hang around with trying to get in touch with you because they always will. When you have those thoughts, just remember they are only thoughts. When those people come around or try coming back in your life, remind yourself that in order to keep your sobriety, you cannot go back to those old places, people or things that you were familiar with when you were in your addiction and by all means stay away from bad association. Please understand that you are responsible for your own recovery. It may not be an easy task, but when those things that you are familiar with pop back into my life, ask yourself, "How bad do you want to recover?"

Gratitude

God gave me the authority to love, but I had to start with learning how to love myself before I could show the love of the Lord to others. Many people have asked me why am I always so happy? Why do I smile all the time? Why is it that every time you see me, I'm dancing? Well, this book is the answer to all of those questions. I am so grateful to be alive today to share my strengths, hopes, and dreams with others. I am grateful that this is not the end, and that this is only the beginning. I am grateful that God has empowered me with unlimited potential. I am grateful to know that there are no obstacles that cannot be overcome.

I am grateful for my son Bernard Mallory who never stopped loving me after all the things that I've put him through.

I am grateful for my sister Debbie Mallory who supported me throughout my entire journey and never left my side.

I am grateful to my oldest sister, who tricked me into going to the treatment center. She saved my life.

Honestly, this list could go on and on because I have so much to be grateful for.

Lastly,

Something that I have learned is that I have come to appreciate my journey. The journey that I have been on has really been a learning experience, to say the least. Through all of the struggles that I have had, it has made me into the woman I am today. Even when there is no one around to encourage me, I will continue to encourage myself. I thank God for a second chance.

Today, tomorrow and forever more

God has delivered me from the drugs, guilt, and the shame of my past. I thank you, God, for saving me from myself. My truth has been exposed, and my faith has been redeemed. Today, "The Sound in my Scream has been heard." **I AM FREE**.

"Truly my soul finds rest in God alone; my salvation comes from Him. Truly He alone is my rock and my salvation; He is my fortress, I will never be shaken." (Psalm. 62:1–2, NIV).

Chapter 7

Trust the Process

The Twelve Steps of Narcotics Anonymous

1. We admitted that we were powerless over our addiction, that our lives had become unmanageable.

2. We came to believe that a Power greater than ourselves could restore us to sanity.

3. We made a decision to turn our will and our lives over to the care of God as we understood Him.

4. We made a searching and fearless moral inventory of ourselves.

5. We admitted to God, to ourselves, and to another human being the exact nature of our wrongs.

6. We were entirely ready to have God remove all these defects of character.

7. We humbly asked Him to remove our shortcomings.

8. We made a list of all persons we had harmed, and became willing to make amends to them all.

9. We made direct amends to such people wherever possible, except when to do so would injure them or others.

10. We continued to take personal inventory and when we were wrong promptly admitted it.

11. We sought through prayer and meditation to improve our conscious contact with God as we understood Him, praying only for the knowledge of His will for us and the power to carry that out.

12. Having had a spiritual awakening as a result of these steps, we tried to carry this message to addicts and to practice these principles in all our affairs.

Did you know?

According to https://www.addictioncenter.com/, Almost 21 million Americans have at least one addiction, yet only 10% of them receive treatment.

Drug overdose deaths have more than tripled since 1990.

From 1999 to 2017, more than 700,000 Americans died from overdosing on a drug.

Every year, worldwide, alcohol is the cause of 5.3% of deaths (or 1 in every 20).

On average, 30 Americans die every day in an alcohol-related car accident, and six Americans die every day from alcohol poisoning.

About 88,000 people die as a result of alcohol every year in the United States.

About 130 Americans die every day from an opiate overdose.

From 1999 to 2017, 399,230 Americans lost their lives to opiates.

About 494,000 Americans over the age of 12 are regular heroin users.

In 2017, 886,000 Americans used heroin at least once.

About 25% of people who try heroin will become addicted.

In 2017, 81,000 Americans tried heroin for the first time.

Over 15,000 Americans died from a heroin overdose in 2017.

About 30-40 million Americans smoke marijuana every year.

About 43% of American adults admit to trying marijuana.

About 5 million Americans are regular cocaine users.

Cocaine was involved in 1 out of every 5 overdose deaths

About 774,000 Americans are regular meth users. About 16,000 of them are between the ages of 12 and 17.

About 10,000 Americans who regularly used meth suffered a fatal overdose in 2017.

About 964,000 Americans are addicted to meth.

SAMHSA National Helpline

Confidential free help, from public health agencies, to find substance use treatment and information.

1-800-662-4357

You can find more information about the 12 step program and the Narcotics Anonymous Basic text

https://12step.org/references/12-step-versions/na/

Check out more statics on drug abuse

https://www.addictioncenter.com/

Scriptures are from the NIV Bible

Substance Use and Mental Healthnimh.nih.gov

My Prayer

I pray that this book will set someone free to do what God has intended them to do. Whether it's to write your own book, to think twice before making bad decisions, to be delivered from fear, to rekindle your marriage, to love your parents, to love your children, to love yourself, and to never take life for granted, I pray that you understand that whatever you've gone through in your past will not determine your future as long as you don't allow it to. I pray that God gives you the strength to endure any adversity that you may ever encounter. I pray that you have joy and happiness. I pray for prosperity in your life. In Jesus name, Amen.

"Seek the Lord and His strength; seek His presence continually!"
(1 Chronicles 16:11, ESV).

About the Author

"I wait quietly before God, for my victory comes from Him. He alone is my rock and my salvation, my fortress where I will never be shaken..."- Ps. 62:1-2 NIV

Kimberly Mallory is an author, educator, motivational speaker and servant of God. She is also a recovering drug addict with a passion for helping others. Her 16 year battle against her drug addiction led her into many dark places and there were times when Kimberly did not know if she would survive the burden. But a  calling from the Lord changed all of that. With His help she turned her life around, rid herself of the drugs that were destroying her and has never once looked back. Now, 17 years after beating her addiction, Kimberly teaches the program of Recovery to women inmates at the Oakland County Jail and leads NA meetings and bible study groups, helping women with addiction to see that there is a way to redemption and a way to save themselves. In addition to that she has written her first book, which is aimed at helping addicts to understand that their past need not determine their future and that addictions can be overcome when you place your trust in God. Kimberly is a regular church-goer and is living testament that you are never too old to learn, having gained her Theology degree in her late fifties. She speaks regularly at women's conferences, conventions, summits and churches, sharing her own experiences with diverse audiences. She also gives back to her community by volunteering at hospitals and hospice centers as a First Responder Lt. Chaplain. Are you able to work with any of these pictures this is for the about the author section also the copy right page has to go in behind the title page.

You may reach Kimberly via email at kimfouchia@gmail.com

Made in the USA
Columbia, SC
30 August 2023

22279196R00039